The Americanism of

Henry Van Dyke

Alpha Editions

This edition published in 2024

ISBN : 9789366387789

Design and Setting By
Alpha Editions
www.alphaedis.com
Email - info@alphaedis.com

As per information held with us this book is in Public Domain.
This book is a reproduction of an important historical work. Alpha Editions uses the best technology to reproduce historical work in the same manner it was first published to preserve its original nature. Any marks or number seen are left intentionally to preserve its true form.

Contents

THE AMERICANISM OF WASHINGTON ....- 1 -

THE AMERICANISM OF WASHINGTON

BY: HENRY VAN DYKE

Hard is the task of the man who at this late day attempts to say anything new about Washington. But perhaps it may be possible to unsay some of the things which have been said, and which, though they were at one time new, have never at any time been strictly true.

The character of Washington, emerging splendid from the dust and tumult of those great conflicts in which he played the leading part, has passed successively into three media of obscurity, from each of which his figure, like the sun shining through vapors, has received some disguise of shape and color. First came the mist of mythology, in which we discerned the new St. George, serene, impeccable, moving through an orchard of ever-blooming cherry-trees, gracefully vanquishing dragons with a touch, and shedding fragrance and radiance around him. Out of that mythological mist we groped our way, to find ourselves beneath the rolling clouds of oratory, above which the head of the hero was pinnacled in remote grandeur, like a sphinx poised upon a volcanic peak, isolated and mysterious. That altitudinous figure still dominates the cloudy landscapes of the after-dinner orator; but the frigid, academic mind has turned away from it, and looking through the fog of criticism has descried another Washington, not really an American, not amazingly a hero, but a very decent English country gentleman, honorable, courageous, good, shrewd, slow, and above all immensely lucky.

Now here are two of the things often said about Washington which need, if I mistake not, to be unsaid: first, that he was a solitary and inexplicable phenomenon of greatness; and second, that he was not an American.

Solitude, indeed, is the last quality that an intelligent student of his career would ascribe to him. Dignified and reserved he was, undoubtedly; and as this manner was natural to him, he won more true friends by using it than if he had disguised himself in a forced familiarity and worn his heart upon his sleeve. But from first to last he was a man who did his work in the bonds of companionship, who trusted his comrades in the great enterprise even though they were not his intimates, and who neither sought nor occupied a lonely eminence of unshared glory. He was not of the jealous race of those who

"Bear, like the Turk, no brother near the throne";

nor of the temper of George III., who chose his ministers for their vacuous compliancy. Washington was surrounded by men of similar though not of equal strength—Franklin, Hamilton, Knox, Greene, the Adamses, Jefferson, Madison. He stands in history not as a lonely pinnacle like Mount Shasta, elevated above the plain

"By drastic lift of pent volcanic fires";

but as the central summit of a mountain range, with all his noble fellowship of kindred peaks about him, enhancing his unquestioned supremacy by their glorious neighborhood and their great support.

Among these men whose union in purpose and action made the strength and stability of the republic, Washington was first, not only in the largeness of his nature, the loftiness of his desires, and the vigor of his will, but also in that representative quality which makes a man able to stand as the true hero of a great people. He had an instinctive power to divine, amid the confusions of rival interests and the cries of factional strife, the new aims and hopes, the vital needs and aspirations, which were the common inspiration of the people's cause and the creative forces of the American nation. The power to understand this, the faith to believe in it, and the unselfish courage to live for it, was the central factor of Washington's life, the heart and fountain of his splendid Americanism.

It was denied during his lifetime, for a little while, by those who envied his greatness, resented his leadership, and sought to shake him from his lofty place. But he stood serene and imperturbable, while that denial, like many another blast of evil-scented wind, passed into nothingness, even before the disappearance of the party strife out of whose fermentation it had arisen. By the unanimous judgment of his countrymen for two generations after his death he was hailed as *Pater Patriae*; and the age which conferred that title was too ingenuous to suppose that the father could be of a different race from his own offspring.

But the modern doubt is more subtle, more curious, more refined in its methods. It does not spring, as the old denial did, from a partisan hatred, which would seek to discredit Washington by an accusation of undue partiality for England, and thus to break his hold upon the love of the people. It arises, rather, like a creeping exhalation, from a modern theory of what true Americanism really is: a theory which goes back, indeed, for its inspiration to Dr. Johnson's somewhat crudely expressed opinion that "the Americans were a race whom no other mortals could wish to resemble"; but which, in its later form, takes counsel with those British connoisseurs who demand of their typical American not depravity of morals but deprivation of manners, not vice of heart but vulgarity of speech, not badness but bumptiousness, and at least enough of eccentricity to make him amusing to cultivated people.

Not a few of our native professors and critics are inclined to accept some features of this view, perhaps in mere reaction from the unamusing character of their own existence. They are not quite ready to subscribe to Mr. Kipling's statement that the real American is

"Unkempt, disreputable, vast,"

I remember reading somewhere that Tennyson had an idea that Longfellow, when he met him, would put his feet upon the table. And it is precisely because Longfellow kept his feet in their proper place, in society as well as in verse, that some critics, nowadays, would have us believe that he was not a truly American poet.

Traces of this curious theory of Americanism in its application to Washington may now be found in many places. You shall hear historians describe him as a transplanted English commoner, a second edition of John Hampden. You shall read, in a famous poem, of Lincoln as

"New birth of our new soil, the *first* American."

He knew it, I say: and by what divination? By a test more searching than any mere peculiarity of manners, dress, or speech; by a touchstone able to divide the gold of essential character from the alloy of superficial characteristics; by a standard which disregarded alike Franklin's fur cap and Putnam's old felt hat, Morgan's leather leggings and Witherspoon's black silk gown and John Adams's lace ruffles, to recognize and approve, beneath these various garbs, the vital sign of America woven into the very souls of the men who belonged to her by a spiritual birthright.

For what is true Americanism, and where does it reside? Not on the tongue, nor in the clothes, nor among the transient social forms, refined or rude, which mottle the surface of human life. The log cabin has no monopoly of it, nor is it an immovable fixture of the stately pillared mansion. Its home is not on the frontier nor in the populous city, not among the trees of the wild forest nor the cultured groves of Academe. Its dwelling is in the heart. It speaks a score of dialects but one language, follows a hundred paths to the same goal, performs a thousand kinds of service in loyalty to the same ideal which is its life. True Americanism is this:

To believe that the inalienable rights of man to life, liberty, and the pursuit of happiness are given by God.

To believe that any form of power that tramples on these rights is unjust.

To believe that taxation without representation is tyranny, that government must rest upon the consent of the governed, and that the people should choose their own rulers.

To believe that freedom must be safeguarded by law and order, and that the end of freedom is fair play for all.

To believe not in a forced equality of conditions and estates, but in a true equalization of burdens, privileges, and opportunities.

To believe that the selfish interests of persons, classes, and sections must be subordinated to the welfare of the commonwealth.

To believe that union is as much a human necessity as liberty is a divine gift.

To believe, not that all people are good, but that the way to make them better is to trust the whole people.

To believe that a free state should offer an asylum to the oppressed, and an example of virtue, sobriety, and fair dealing to all nations.

To believe that for the existence and perpetuity of such a state a man should be willing to give his whole service, in property, in labor, and in life.

That is Americanism; an ideal embodying itself in a people; a creed heated white hot in the furnace of conviction and hammered into shape on the anvil of life; a vision commanding men to follow it whithersoever it may lead them. And it was the subordination of the personal self to that ideal, that creed, that vision, which gave eminence and glory to Washington and the men who stood with him.

This is the truth that emerges, crystalline and luminous, from the conflicts and confusions of the Revolution. The men who were able to surrender themselves and all their interests to the pure and loyal service of their ideal were the men who made good, the victors crowned with glory and honor. The men who would not make that surrender, who sought selfish ends, who were controlled by personal ambition and the love of gain, who were willing to stoop to crooked means to advance their own fortunes, were the failures, the lost leaders, and, in some cases, the men whose names are embalmed in their own infamy. The ultimate secret of greatness is neither physical nor intellectual, but moral. It is the capacity to lose self in the service of something greater. It is the faith to recognize, the will to obey, and the strength to follow, a star.

Washington, no doubt, was pre-eminent among his contemporaries in natural endowments. Less brilliant in his mental gifts than some, less eloquent and accomplished than others, he had a rare balance of large powers which justified Lowell's phrase of "an imperial man." His athletic vigor and skill, his steadiness of nerve restraining an intensity of passion, his undaunted courage which refused no necessary risks and his prudence which took no unnecessary ones, the quiet sureness with which he grasped large ideas and the pressing energy with which he executed small details, the breadth of his intelligence, the depth of his convictions, his power to apply great thoughts and principles to every-day affairs, and his singular superiority to current prejudices and illusions—these were gifts in combination which would have made him distinguished in any company, in any age.

But what was it that won and kept a free field for the exercise of these gifts? What was it that secured for them a long, unbroken opportunity of development in the activities of leadership, until they reached the summit of their perfection? It was a moral quality. It was the evident magnanimity of the man, which assured the people that he was no self-seeker who would betray their interests for his own glory or rob them for his own gain. It was the supreme magnanimity of the man, which made the best spirits of the time trust him implicitly, in war and peace, as one who would never forget his duty or his integrity in the sense of his own greatness.

From the first, Washington appears not as a man aiming at prominence or power, but rather as one under obligation to serve a cause. Necessity was laid upon him, and he met it willingly. After Washington's marvellous escape from death in his first campaign for the defence of the colonies, the Rev. Samuel Davies, fourth president of Princeton College, spoke of him in a sermon as "that heroic youth, Colonel Washington, whom I can but hope Providence has hitherto preserved in so signal a manner for some important service to his country." It was a prophetic voice, and Washington was not disobedient to the message. Chosen to command the Army of the Revolution in 1775, he confessed to his wife his deep reluctance to surrender the joys of home, acknowledged publicly his feeling that he was not equal to the great trust committed to him, and then, accepting it as thrown upon him "by a kind of destiny," he gave himself body and soul to its fulfilment refusing all pay beyond the mere discharge of his expenses, of which he kept a strict account, and asking no other reward than the success of the cause which he served.

"Ah, but he was a rich man," cries the carping critic; "he could afford to do it." How many rich men to-day avail themselves of their opportunity to indulge in this kind of extravagance, toiling tremendously without a salary, neglecting their own estate for the public benefit, seeing their property diminished without complaint, and coming into serious financial embarrassment, even within sight of bankruptcy, as Washington did, merely for the gratification of a desire to serve the people? This is indeed a very singular and noble form of luxury. But the wealth which makes it possible neither accounts for its existence nor detracts from its glory. It is the fruit of a manhood superior alike to riches and to poverty, willing to risk all, and to use all, for the common good.

Was it in any sense a misfortune for the people of America, even the poorest among them, that there was a man able to advance sixty-four thousand dollars out of his own purse, with no other security but his own faith in their cause, to pay his daily expenses while he was leading their armies? This unsecured loan was one of the very things, I doubt not, that helped to inspire general confidence. Even so the prophet Jeremiah purchased a field in Anathoth, in the days when Judah was captive unto Babylon, paying down the money, seventeen shekels of silver, as a token of his faith that the land would some day be delivered from the enemy and restored to peaceful and orderly habitation.

Washington's substantial pledge of property to the cause of liberty was repaid by a grateful country at the close of the war. But not a dollar of payment for the tremendous toil of body and mind, not a dollar for work "overtime," for indirect damages to his estate, for commissions on the benefits which he secured for the general enterprise, for the use of his name or the value of his counsel, would he receive.

A few years later, when his large sagacity perceived that the development of internal commerce was one of the first needs of the new country, at a time when he held no public office, he became president of a company for the extension of navigation on the rivers James and Potomac. The Legislature of Virginia proposed to give him a hundred and fifty shares of stock. Washington refused this, or any other kind of pay, saying that he could serve the people better in the enterprise if he were known to have no selfish interest in it. He was not the kind of a man to reconcile himself to a gratuity (which is the Latinized word for a "tip" offered to a person not in livery), and if the modern methods of "coming in on the ground-floor" and "taking a rake-off" had been explained and suggested to him, I suspect that he would have described them in language more notable for its force than for its elegance.

It is true, of course, that the fortune which he so willingly imperilled and impaired recouped itself again after peace was established, and his industry and wisdom made him once more a rich man for those days. But what injustice was there in that? It is both natural and right that men who have risked their all to secure for the country at large what they could have secured for themselves by other means, should share in the general prosperity attendant upon the success of their efforts and sacrifices for the common good.

I am sick of the shallow judgment that ranks the worth of a man by his poverty or by his wealth at death. Many a selfish speculator dies poor. Many an unselfish patriot dies prosperous. It is not the possession of the dollar that cankers the soul, it is the worship of it. The true test of a man is this: Has he labored for his own interest, or for the general welfare? Has he earned his money fairly or unfairly? Does he use it greedily or generously? What does it mean to him, a personal advantage over his fellow-men, or a personal opportunity of serving them?

There are a hundred other points in Washington's career in which the same supremacy of character, magnanimity focussed on service to an ideal, is revealed in conduct. I see it in the wisdom with which he, a son of the South, chose most of his generals from the North, that he might secure immediate efficiency and unity in the army. I see it in the generosity with which he praised the achievements of his associates, disregarding jealous rivalries, and ever willing to share the credit of victory as he was to bear the burden of defeat. I see it in the patience with which he suffered his fame to be imperilled for the moment by reverses and retreats, if only he might the more surely guard the frail hope of ultimate victory for his country. I see it in the quiet dignity with which he faced the Conway Cabal, not anxious to defend his own reputation and secure his own power, but nobly resolute to save the army from being crippled and the cause of liberty from being wrecked. I see it in the splendid self-forgetfulness which cleansed his mind of all temptation to take personal revenge upon those who had sought to injure him in that base intrigue. I read it in his letter of consolation and encouragement to the wretched Gates after the defeat at Camden. I hear the prolonged reechoing music of it in his letter to General Knox in 1798, in regard to military appointments, declaring his wish to "avoid feuds with those who are embarked in the same general enterprise with myself."

Listen to the same spirit as it speaks in his circular address to the governors of the different States, urging them to "forget their local prejudices and policies; to make those mutual concessions which are requisite to the general prosperity, and in some instances to sacrifice their individual advantages to the interest of the community." Watch how it guides him unerringly through the critical period of American history which lies between the success of the Revolution and the establishment of the nation, enabling him to avoid the pitfalls of sectional and partisan strife, and to use his great influence with the people in leading them out of the confusion of a weak confederacy into the strength of an indissoluble union of sovereign States.

See how he once more sets aside his personal preferences for a quiet country life, and risks his already secure popularity, together with his reputation for consistency, by obeying the voice which calls him to be a candidate for the Presidency. See how he chooses for the cabinet and for the Supreme Court, not an exclusive group of personal friends, but men who can be trusted to serve the great cause of Union with fidelity and power—Jefferson, Randolph, Hamilton, Knox, John Jay, Wilson, Cushing, Rutledge. See how patiently and indomitably he gives himself to the toil of office, deriving from his exalted station no gain "beyond the lustre which may be reflected from its connection with a power of promoting human felicity." See how he retires, at last, to the longed-for joys of private life, confessing that his career has not been without errors of judgment, beseeching the Almighty that they may bring no harm to his country, and asking no other reward for his labors than to partake, "in the midst of my fellow-citizens, the benign influence of good laws under a free government, the ever favorite object of my heart."

Oh, sweet and stately words, revealing, through their calm reserve, the inmost secret of a life that did not flare with transient enthusiasm but glowed with unquenchable devotion to a cause! "The ever favorite object of my heart"—how quietly, how simply he discloses the source and origin of a sublime consecration, a lifelong heroism! Thus speaks the victor in calm retrospect of the long battle. But if you would know the depth and the intensity of the divine fire that burned within his breast you must go back to the dark and icy days of Valley Forge, and hear him cry in passion unrestrained: "If I know my own mind, I could offer myself a living sacrifice to the butchering enemy, provided that would contribute to the people's ease. I would be a living offering to the savage fury and die by inches to save the people."

"*The ever favorite object of my heart*!" I strike this note again and again, insisting upon it, harping upon it; for it is the key-note of the music. It is the capacity to find such an object in the success of the people's cause, to follow it unselfishly, to serve it loyally, that distinguishes the men who stood with Washington and who deserve to share his fame. I read the annals of the Revolution, and I find everywhere this secret and searching test dividing the strong from the weak, the noble from the base, the heirs of glory from the captives of oblivion and the inheritors of shame. It was the unwillingness to sink and forget self in the service of something greater that made the failures and wrecks of those tempestuous times, through which the single-hearted and the devoted pressed on to victory and honor.

Turn back to the battle of Saratoga. There were two Americans on that field who suffered under a great personal disappointment: Philip Schuyler, who was unjustly supplanted in command of the army by General Gates; and Benedict Arnold, who was deprived by envy of his due share in the glory of winning the battle. Schuyler forgot his own injury in loyalty to the cause, offered to serve Gates in any capacity, and went straight on to the end of his noble life giving all that he had to his country. But in Arnold's heart the favorite object was not his country, but his own ambition, and the wound which his pride received at Saratoga rankled and festered and spread its poison through his whole nature, until he went forth from the camp, "a leper white as snow."

What was it that made Charles Lee, as fearless a man as ever lived, play the part of a coward in order to hide his treason at the battle of Monmouth? It was the inward eating corruption of that selfish vanity which caused him to desire the defeat of an army whose command he had wished but failed to attain. He had offered his sword to America for his own glory, and when that was denied him, he withdrew the offering, and died, as he had lived, to himself.

What was it that tarnished the fame of Gates and Wilkinson and Burr and Conway? What made their lives, and those of men like them, futile and inefficient compared with other men whose natural gifts were less? It was the taint of dominant selfishness that ran through their careers, now hiding itself, now breaking out in some act of malignity or treachery. Of the common interest they were reckless, provided they might advance their own. Disappointed in that "ever favorite object of their hearts," they did not hesitate to imperil the cause in whose service they were enlisted.

Turn to other cases, in which a charitable judgment will impute no positive betrayal of trusts, but a defect of vision to recognize the claim of the higher ideal. Tory or Revolutionist a man might be, according to his temperament and conviction; but where a man begins with protests against tyranny and ends with subservience to it, we look for the cause. What was it that separated Joseph Galloway from Francis Hopkinson? It was Galloway's opinion that, while the struggle for independence might be justifiable, it could not be successful, and the temptation of a larger immediate reward under the British crown than could ever be given by the American Congress in which he had once served. What was it that divided the Rev. Jacob Duché from the Rev. John Witherspoon? It was Duché's fear that the cause for which he had prayed so eloquently in the first Continental Congress was doomed after the capture of Philadelphia, and his unwillingness to go down with that cause instead of enjoying the comfortable fruits of his native wit and eloquence in an easy London chaplaincy. What was it that cut William Franklin off from his professedly prudent and worldly wise old father, Benjamin? It was the luxurious and benumbing charm of the royal governorship of New Jersey.

"Professedly prudent" is the phrase that I have chosen to apply to Benjamin Franklin. For the one thing that is clear, as we turn to look at him and the other men who stood with Washington, is that, whatever their philosophical professions may have been, they were not controlled by prudence. They were really imprudent, and at heart willing to take all risks of poverty and death in a struggle whose cause was just though its issue was dubious. If it be rashness to commit honor and life and property to a great adventure for the general good, then these men were rash to the verge of recklessness. They refused no peril, they withheld no sacrifice, in the following of their ideal.

I hear John Dickinson saying: "It is not our duty to leave wealth to our children, but it is our duty to leave liberty to them. We have counted the cost of this contest, and we find nothing so dreadful as voluntary slavery." I see Samuel Adams, impoverished, living upon a pittance, hardly able to provide a decent coat for his back, rejecting with scorn the offer of a profitable office, wealth, a title even, to win him from his allegiance to the cause of America. I see Robert Morris, the wealthy merchant, opening his purse and pledging his credit to support the Revolution, and later devoting all his fortune and his energy to restore and establish the financial honor of the Republic, with the memorable words, "The United States may command all that I have, except my integrity." I hear the proud John Adams saying to his wife, "I have accepted a seat in the House of Representatives, and thereby have consented to my own ruin, to your ruin, and the ruin of our children"; and I hear her reply, with the tears running down her face, "Well, I am willing in this cause to run all risks with you, and be ruined with you, if you are ruined," I see Benjamin Franklin, in the Congress of 1776, already past his seventieth year, prosperous, famous, by far the most celebrated man in America, accepting without demur the difficult and dangerous mission to France, and whispering to his friend, Dr. Rush, "I am old and good for nothing, but as the store-keepers say of their remnants of cloth, 'I am but a fag-end, and you may have me for what you please.'"

Here is a man who will illustrate and prove, perhaps better than any other of those who stood with Washington, the point at which I am aiming. There was none of the glamour of romance about old Ben Franklin. He was shrewd, canny, humorous. The chivalric Southerners disliked his philosophy, and the solemn New-Englanders mistrusted his jokes. He made no extravagant claims for his own motives, and some of his ways were not distinctly ideal. He was full of prudential proverbs, and claimed to be a follower of the theory of enlightened self-interest. But there was not a faculty of his wise old head which he did not put at the service of his country, nor was there a pulse of his slow and steady heart which did not beat loyal to the cause of freedom.

He forfeited profitable office and sure preferment under the crown, for hard work, uncertain pay, and certain peril in behalf of the colonies. He followed the inexorable logic, step by step, which led him from the natural rights of his countrymen to their liberty, from their liberty to their independence. He endured with a grim humor the revilings of those whom he called "malevolent critics and bug-writers." He broke with his old and dear associates in England, writing to one of them,

"You and I were long friends; you are now my enemy and I am Yours,

B. Franklin."

He never flinched or faltered at any sacrifice of personal ease or interest to the demands of his country. His patient, skilful, laborious efforts in France did as much for the final victory of the American cause as any soldier's sword. He yielded his own opinions in regard to the method of making the treaty of peace with England, and thereby imperilled for a time his own prestige. He served as president of Pennsylvania three times, devoting all his salary to public benefactions. His influence in the Constitutional Convention was steadfast on the side of union and harmony, though in many things he differed from the prevailing party. His voice was among those who hailed Washington as the only possible candidate for the Presidency. His last public act was a petition to Congress for the abolition of slavery. At his death the government had not yet settled his accounts in its service, and his country was left apparently his debtor; which, in a sense still larger and deeper, she must remain as long as liberty endures and union triumphs in the Republic.

Is not this, after all, the root of the whole matter? Is not this the thing that is vitally and essentially true of all those great men, clustering about Washington, whose fame we honor and revere with his? They all left the community, the commonwealth, the race, in debt to them. This was their purpose and the ever-favorite object of their hearts. They were deliberate and joyful creditors. Renouncing the maxim of worldly wisdom which bids men "get all you can and keep all you get," they resolved rather to give all they had to advance the common cause, to use every benefit conferred upon them in the service of the general welfare, to bestow upon the world more than they received from it, and to leave a fair and unblotted account of business done with life which should show a clear balance in their favor.

Thus, in brief outline, and in words which seem poor and inadequate, I have ventured to interpret anew the story of Washington and the men who stood with him: not as a stirring ballad of battle and danger, in which the knights ride valiantly, and are renowned for their mighty strokes at the enemy in arms; not as a philosophic epic, in which the development of a great national idea is displayed, and the struggle of opposing policies is traced to its conclusion; but as a drama of the eternal conflict in the soul of man between self-interest in its Protean forms, and loyalty to the right, service to a cause, allegiance to an ideal.

Those great actors who played in it have passed away, but the same drama still holds the stage. The drop-curtain falls between the acts; the scenery shifts; the music alters; but the crisis and its issues are unchanged, and the parts which you and I play are assigned to us by our own choice of "the ever favorite object of our hearts."

Men tell us that the age of ideals is past, and that we are now come to the age of expediency, of polite indifference to moral standards, of careful attention to the bearing of different policies upon our own personal interests. Men tell us that the rights of man are a poetic fiction, that democracy has nothing in it to command our allegiance unless it promotes our individual comfort and prosperity, and that the whole duty of a citizen is to vote with his party and get an office for himself, or for some one who will look after him. Men tell us that to succeed means to get money, because with that all other good things can be secured. Men tell us that the one thing to do is to promote and protect the particular trade, or industry, or corporation in which we have a share: the laws of trade will work out that survival of the fittest which is the only real righteousness, and if we survive that will prove that we are fit. Men tell us that all beyond this is phantasy, dreaming, Sunday-school politics: there is nothing worth living for except to get on in the world; and nothing at all worth dying for, since the age of ideals is past.

It is past indeed for those who proclaim, or whisper, or in their hearts believe, or in their lives obey, this black gospel. And what is to follow? An age of cruel and bitter jealousies between sections and classes; of hatted and strife between the Haves and the Have-nots; of futile contests between parties which have kept their names and confused their principles, so that no man may distinguish them except as the Ins and Outs. An age of greedy privilege and sullen poverty, of blatant luxury and curious envy, of rising palaces and vanishing homes, of stupid frivolity and idiotic publicomania; in which four hundred gilded fribbles give monkey-dinners and Louis XV. revels, while four million ungilded gossips gape at them and read about them in the newspapers. An age when princes of finance buy protection from the representatives of a fierce democracy; when guardians of the savings which insure the lives of the poor, use them as a surplus to pay for the extravagances of the rich; and when men who have climbed above their fellows on golden ladders, tremble at the crack of the blackmailer's whip and come down at the call of an obscene newspaper. An age when the python of political corruption casts its "rings" about the neck of proud cities and sovereign States, and throttles honesty to silence and liberty to death. It is such an age, dark, confused, shameful, that the sceptic and the scorner must face, when they turn their backs upon those ancient shrines where the flames of faith and integrity and devotion are flickering like the deserted altar-fires of a forsaken worship.

But not for us who claim our heritage in blood and spirit from Washington and the men who stood with him,—not for us of other tribes and kindred who

"Have found a fatherland upon this shore,"

and learned the meaning of manhood beneath the shelter of liberty,—not for us, nor for our country, that dark apostasy, that dismal outlook! We see the palladium of the American ideal—goddess of the just eye, the unpolluted heart, the equal hand—standing as the image of Athene stood above the upper streams of Simois:

"It stood, and sun and moonshine rained their light

On the pure columns of its glen-built hall.

Backward and forward rolled the waves of fight

Round Troy—but while this stood Troy could not fall."

We see the heroes of the present conflict, the men whose allegiance is not to sections but to the whole people, the fearless champions of fair play. We hear from the chair of Washington a brave and honest voice which cries that our industrial problems must be solved not in the interest of capital, nor of labor, but of the whole people. We believe that the liberties which the heroes of old won with blood and sacrifice are ours to keep with labor and service.

"All that our fathers wrought With true prophetic thought, Must be

defended."

No privilege that encroaches upon those liberties is to be endured. No lawless disorder that imperils them is to be sanctioned. No class that disregards or invades them is to be tolerated.

There is a life that is worth living now, as it was worth living in the former days, and that is the honest life, the useful life, the unselfish life, cleansed by devotion to an ideal. There is a battle that is worth fighting now, as it was worth fighting then, and that is the battle for justice and equality. To make our city and our State free in fact as well as in name; to break the rings that strangle real liberty, and to keep them broken; to cleanse, so far as in our power lies, the fountains of our national life from political, commercial, and social corruption; to teach our sons and daughters, by precept and example, the honor of serving such a country as America—that is work worthy of the finest manhood and womanhood. The well born are those who are born to do that work. The well bred are those who are bred to be proud of that work. The well educated are those who see deepest into the meaning and the necessity of that work. Nor shall their labor be for naught, nor the reward of their sacrifice fail them. For high in the firmament of human destiny are set the stars of faith in mankind, and unselfish courage, and loyalty to the ideal; and while they shine, the Americanism of Washington and the men who stood with him shall never, never die.

THE END